HEAD T OF THE TERRIER

G000129173

Poems Of Life With A Terrier

Alexia Muelle-Rushbrook

Written in the UK 2020

Written by Alexia Muelle-Rushbrook

Photographs by Alexia Muelle-Rushbrook

ISBN 978-1-911311-81-2

I dedicate this book to all the terriers.
May us mere humans deserve you.

To my Mum; who knew I took after you a little, after all?
I'm just sorry I realised it too late for you to read this.

To Dad; For enabling the terrier dream - and so much more!

To all the Ladies, Gentlemen and Furbabies of Wederdena – you know who you are.
Thank you!

Long Live The Terrier!

1. INTRODUCTION

Head to Tail

To appreciate the terrier
From head to tail
That is the aim within
I hope it does not fail

I'll do my best to express the love
The loyalty and of course the fun
Every minute that you know them
Your heart will eternally be won

But if you think them simple
Or over them you can easily win
Then you need to read on
And pay close attention!

For the cheek has no limit
Thankfully the charm has no bound
The like of a terrier
Absolutely cannot be found!

If you have a terrier
I think you'll understand
And be relieved to know
That you're not alone in this land!

We can all be baffled
Amused and obsessed
With the cheek, the charm
The never-ending happiness

That spirit that is unwavering
The joy that improves every mood
That ability to get into mischief
As if they have something to prove!

Long live the terrier!
Understand them if you can
Love and cherish them forever
As in this book I am

The Point Is

To educate the humans
With whom I spend my life
To show them what it is to live with us
Come whatever might

To realise there is no point
In taking things so seriously
To learn a little humour
To adore all about me!

To understand that not everything
Together must make sense
But in the highs and lows of life
Together we will not repent

For every step is easier
When walked with the likes of me
You may call me a 'cheeky lump'
I call me 'made perfectly'

So, while you try to make sense
To understand from head to tail
I tell you I am already there
It's not my fault you understand like a snail!

I will try to educate you
Or at least try to teach you to say
'Ok, I just misunderstood
Let's get on with the day!'

Terrier Clout

I do not share
I do not shout
I express myself
With terrier clout
That is imparting knowledge
With finesse
Join me, won't you
We're the best!

2. OBSERVATIONS OF LIFE WITH A TERRIER

Silence Is Golden

Whoever said 'Silence is Golden'
Obviously had a cat
For anyone with a dog
Would never say that!

Silence *is* suspicious
And contains a threat
Mischief unspoken
Damage not found yet!

Silence is golden?!
Ha, that's a joke!
I prefer a gentle movement
So no evil thoughts provoke!

Fear of the carnage
That's bound to befall
Once that silence is broken
And I see all!

For seeing dispels
Any real doubt
That silence was in fact
Just a prelude to a shout

Or the sudden realisation
That the soft gentle crunch
Is in fact, not
The eating of lunch

But the gentle destruction
That some object left
Has gained the affection
At which, no one will jest

Tragedy has befallen
Death has become
Some object once cherished
Now bears the brunt of their fun!

Cute

What is cute
How does it define?
How does it get away
With countless crime?

It has the ability
To wash away
Any filthy mess
As clear as day

Just one look
And I will forget
And won't stop
To regret

Any misdemeanour
Is no more
No wrong here
Just amour!

Cuteness all around
Does say
"I am cute, with everything
I can get away!"

Sweet Song

I'm not sure how to spell it
That little sound of glee
The song you sing as a greeting
A way of calling me
But it melts the heart every time
To gain attention, it never fails
Who could ignore, such a sweet song?
That comes with such happy, wagging tails?

Discovery

When I see you in the distance
Tail wagging as fast
As a mill in a strong wind
I know a critter isn't going to last

A trail has been discovered
A hole has been undug
Someone's peace is disturbed
And I doubt you'll just give it a hug!

Bottoms Up!

When bottoms are up
And heads are down
Something is crawling
Something they've found

Some little critter
Their attention has gained
Some little critter
Is about to be claimed!

Angel

You know when you heard a strange noise
You went to have a look?
But when you get there
Your pup looks textbook!?

Nothing out of place
Nothing you can *see*!
But deep down you know
It's only a matter of time for transparency

Something *did* just happen
But your pup is no fool
She has 'puppy eyes' down to a T
And knows exactly how to use those tools!

A surprise is hidden
In some cheeky way
You can only hope it's a good one
But experience says, nay!

The chances of destruction
Or even a little poo
Are much higher than
An actual gift for you!

It's a good job she's adorable!
She knows that only too well
That she'll get away with everything
She's a little Angel, can't you tell?!

Motto

A motto to live by
And repeat whilst in bed
'Let sleeping dogs lie'
No truer words are said
For while they are sleeping
All around is good
No mischief in the making
Except in the dream neighbourhood

Do not underestimate
The depth of that sleep
For they keep an eye open
Or so it would seem
Ready to jump up
The moment that you move
Their loyalty unbreaking
And ever ready to prove

Or ready just in case
A game is about to start
They will not miss out
They absolutely must take part
Or go out for a walk
Or help make tea
Whatever I am doing
They're right beside me!

Little Miss Independent

Little Miss Independent
A troublesome one is she
You can try to tame her
But 'good luck' I say to thee

She means absolutely no malice
Only joy is in her way
But boy, will you need a sense of humour
To live with her each day!

She will love a cuddle
A game and time with you
But try to call her when she's not ready
And you'll have a surprise or two

Don't be in a hurry
Or chase after her
For she'll just take longer
And laughter will occur

From her of course, not from you
But a game she *will* find
As fear of trouble or growing anger
Flashes through your mind

You better hope she is a 'foodie'
Otherwise, your game just got worse!
You'll wish the crinkle of a packet
Controlled her universe!

For if not, just blind faith
And a solid hope
That when you try to call or retrieve from her
She doesn't turn around and say 'nope!'

Walk On

Walk on, walk on
With hope in your heart
Your terrier will return
And you won't walk alone to the start!
You saw her on the horizon
You saw the chased tail
You know calling is a waste of breath
That her recall did just fail!

You can only carry on in the hope
That she will tire out or her joy fade
That eventually she will give up
And not actually catch or trade
You for that little fluffy creature
That you did just see
Running for all its worth
As fast as it could be!

Continue in the firm hope
Hold it in your heart
Love will conquer all
And she'll meet you at the start!
You may be irritated
Or maybe a little bemused
Or both in equal measure
It's best to be amused!

She really is a monster
But she knows her name
And here she comes a runnin'
Like she's never been away!
Walk on, walk on
In the knowledge that with a terrier goes
You'll always walk together
Like no one else knows!

Always

You're always beside me
You walk with me each day
Regardless of what I'm doing
Whether it be work, rest or play

Ever ready to be on guard
Or comfort me when I'm sad
Always willing to listen to my woes
And be the one that makes me glad

Together we go places
And enjoy the fresh air
Walking out together
No better way is there

Your quirky personality
Cheers me every time
Who needs blind obedience
When terrier cheek is sublime?

A true test of humour
I wouldn't have it any other way
Once you've had a terrier
You'll understand just what I say

Owner

People say I'm your owner
But that simply isn't true
Some days it's you that owns me
And cheers me, when I'm blue

But neither is a true statement
For it is so much more than that
It's a bond beyond ownership
Or even guardianship, like with a cat

It is a bond, a joining
A new kind of membership
A sharing of beings
An eternal friendship

The making of family
The joining of our days
Sharing fun experiences
And completion of each day

3. REASONING WITH YOUR TERRIER

Ah, to be a Terrier

You drive me quite crazy
No, let's say insane
How is it possible
To completely blank your name?

I know you hear me calling
You know exactly where I am!
Apparently, that's not as interesting
As the neighbours' ram!

Oh, for heaven's sake
Will you just return?
Why won't you come back?
When *will* you learn?

Maybe its *I* that needs the lesson?
By now I should know!
That letting you off the lead
Really is a no, no!

Yes, you come back eventually
With that big infectious smile
And we greet with enthusiasm
But inside I'm going wild!

You'd get away with murder
I'm pretty sure you would!
One smile at the bloomin' judge
And he'd declare you good!

Ah, to be a terrier!
Always right, not wrong!
Come, let's go back home
The place we both belong!

Trip hazard

Your ability to lie around
In an inconvenient place
It is quite amazing
You take up *all* the space!

Do you sit in the corner?
Or in your actual bed?
No, you'd rather be
Smack in the middle instead!

You are not missing
Any action, food or joy
No one will get past you
Without tripping on your toy!

You observe everything
From your position of power
No unseen visitor, postman
Or quick visits to the shower

If anyone trips on you?
Well, that's just their fault
You are clear as day
Laying like a horizontal vault

If only you were as observant
From your cosy little bed!
Maybe I'd trip less
And wouldn't have banged my head!

Enough!

I wish it were the last time
I would have to say
I do not want to know
How many pigeons are here today!

Yes, they are flappy and stupid
But I really do not see
The great advantage
Of shouting up the tree?!

They are just mocking you
Now who's the daft one, hey?
Unless you've learnt a sonic bark?
Just let him get on with his day!

If I hear about that pigeon
One more time today
I really will, go quite nuts
And not be responsible for what I say!

The air will be rather blue
I have really had enough!
I do not care, if it's true
That pigeon isn't tough!

He isn't even bothered!
He just sits in the tree
Minding his own business
That doesn't bother me!

Yes, he may flap and taunt you
But why not rise above?
Try showing forgiveness
And everlasting love!

All Weathers

Through wind and rain
It's all the same
It's playtime apparently

I think it grim
But you can swim
And frolic happily

Surely, we're done?
This really isn't fun!
Tell me how can it be?

We're soaked right through
Not just me, but you
Can't we go back in?

Contrary

You are a contrary Mary!
That is for sure!
If I want you to go out to pee
You can't possibly go out the door!
But oh, if *you* decide to go walkies?
Or if a shadow moves the wrong way
Then we must go out
In wind, rain or come what may!

I protect you from the sun's rays
And keep you in the cool
But when you feel the need
Will you go in the pool?
No! not if I asked you!
Then, you'll just look
But given a muddy puddle
You'll roll 'til you look like a rook!

So yes, I say you are contrary!
For everything has to be your way
But I suppose I wanted character
And I got that, you say?
Ah, yes, I suppose I did!
So, I have no reason to complain?!
So, your Highness, how do you
Wish me to entertain?

Entertainment

I bought you a selection
Of lovely toys
All nice and shiny
Some even make a noise!
But are you interested?
Do you give a fig?
No, you're more interested
In what they're wrapped up in!
Or in my lost sock
Or my old shoe
Or even a new one
It's all the same to you!
A freshly fallen branch
Or something dug up
The more it smells
The happier the pup!
Why do I bother?
How much should I spend?
On entertaining my canine
Hairy-little friend?
Hundreds and thousands
Ah, yes of course!
There's no need
To get buyer's remorse!

Wake up

You wake me up each morning
With amazing skill
No one needs an alarm clock
With you about to instil
Punctuality, into my day
For you do not miss
An opportunity to wake me up
With a great big sloppy kiss

Prime Time

I wish you would let my alarm clock
Do its job once in a while
And not wake me up
In your own crazy style

How *do* you know the time I set?
And when it's five minutes before?
I really haven't got a clue
But you I do implore

Let the alarm ring out!
Let me rest for extra time!
You never know, I might just
Wake up in my prime!

Explain It

I understand you are meant to dig
To hunt along the hedge
To sort out any kind of pest
That you might think I dread
But can you explain it?
Put it simply for me please
Why or how on earth
You need to bark up at the tree?
I'm yet to see a pigeon
Squirrel or even cat
Think "Ah, ok, I'll just drop
Right into his lap"?
No, they are more likely
To stay up in that tree
So how about you try something new
And try stalking silently?!
Wouldn't that be novel?
You know it might just work?!
Rather than give the game away
And run about like a jerk?!
You manage with some rabbit holes
You stalk them patiently
So why on earth, can you not
Do the same with the bloomin' tree?!

In Charge

I see you staring
Waiting for me to make a move
Regardless of my motive
You always need to prove

You observe everything
You always know the time
And do not appreciate
Me messing with your design

For you decide our actions
How dare I suggest?!
That I might be the one in control
And put your wisdom to the test?!

Did You Just Eat That?

Did you just eat that?
Oh, good grief you did!
Anyone would think I don't feed you
As they watch you dig!

Every little insect
Worm and grubby bug
All seem to get your attention
And I doubt it is love!

You even eat feathers
Why, I am not sure?
There's no nutritional value
That can be worth the way you gnaw!

It may remind you of the chicken
Pigeon or whatever bird
You have been stalking
But to eat it is quite absurd!

Then, so is eating flowers
Or bark off the tree
I cannot count how many times
I've issued warnings of splinters, to thee!

But you do not listen!
All must be tested in your mouth
Some you just wobble
Some are swallowed, like that mouse

I understand, it is your way
That's how you learn and get a thrill
Sniffing and digging is fun
But sometimes fear, you do instil!

So, I wish to issue a disclaimer
For all around to see
I actually *do* feed you
Nutritious food, *daily*!!

Lost or Left

Lost it or left it?
I ask you that a lot of the time
That question often does occur
And playtime can define

Mostly you got distracted
But know where the ball lays
But occasionally it would seem
It truly is mislaid

You watch me hoping
I saw where it did land
Either that or you know where it is
And I've yet to understand

The amusement in watching
Me search about
Grumbling to myself
As you act as the look out

Then comes the surprise
You appear though in a dream
Holding that ball
Like a miracle it would seem!

Just moments after I give up
Resigning myself to the fact
Another I'll have to buy
And may as well get a whole new pack

I'm pretty sure you're smiling
Nay, laughing at me
I know I'm the object of your mirth
You cheeky little monkey!

What Are You Doing?

I can't see what you're doing
Or exactly what you've got
But I'm pretty sure I don't like it
So will you please just stop?

Walk away and leave it
Exactly where it is
Keep out of mischief
Try to be a good kid!

No? That is not possible?
Oh, what a shame!
I suppose I should investigate?
Or see who's to blame

Ignore at my peril!
Later I certainly will regret
If I don't investigate
The whereabouts of my pet!

Proclaim

I do not know why you are so loud
I can hear you very well
I do wish you would not shout
And your decibels you would quell!

Try whispering like a gentle river
Brook or even stream
A simple sweet bubbling
Like you do, when you dream!

But no, that cannot be
My ears you must shake!
Just in case I am asleep
And from danger I must awake

Only a stormy sea
Or great thunderstorm
Is enough to replicate
And your message to inform!

I tell you're mistaken
I am standing oh, so near
And I am, in fact close enough
To hear you oh, so clear!

But you are not convinced
The message is the same
If you do not annunciate
And loud and clear proclaim!

Disagree with the Decree

I am aware
You decreed
You should be fed
For that display of speed
Or for that impressive
Party trick
Or for retrieving
That big stick
But you see?
We do *not* agree!
That for every move
Treats are free
Or that I should share
On every request
I am afraid I dare
To suggest
That you're in danger
And will become
A little too chubby
To be able to run!

Grab 'n' Shake

You grab and shake
You do not wait
For it to get away

Inanimate or live
Your joy does thrive
In the way you play

That shimmy 'n' shake
The characteristic wake
That follows in your way

You show who's boss
No one is at a loss
They know a terrier has come to play!

Wood For The Trees

The wood should be on the trees
Not in your bed
Can you let me know
If you don't understand what I said?

Destroying lumps of wood
Dragging in a tree
Is not acceptable
So, will you please just leave

Bark on the branches
Twigs with their leaves
And most of all
Wood with the trees!

Call me old fashioned
But I don't appreciate
Such a dangerous toy
Or your way to decorate

You say I confuse you?
At Christmas I change the rule?
Ah, but then it comes
With roots and all!

And a decorative plant pot
Or even better, if its fake!
Then I don't clean at all
And no tree meets its fate!

You see, they should be outside
Not in the living room
And especially not in pieces
And chewed, so I need a broom!

I hope I've cleared that up
In more ways than one
So why not find a better toy
That won't splinter in your gum!

Jog On

You bark at black Labradors
But not at the neighbour's sheepdog
You hate all cyclists
Or anyone that you see out for a jog
Given the chance
You'll see them off your street
But get a glimpse of a treat packet
And you love everyone you meet!

You arrive everywhere
Like you own it and do reign
Supreme over everything
That you care to name!
You leave reminders
For others who dare to walk
Thereabouts in your domain
I suppose, it's how you talk!

But should you meet a friend
Whilst out and about
You call out to them
With a special shout
And wag and bounce
With heart-warming glee
Whilst us humans watch
And wait for thee

I love to see you frolic
And really enjoy
All that is about you
And even share a toy
But why can't you consider?
Doing the bloomin' same
With the poor jogger
Who you refuse to entertain?

Recall

Ah! At last! I've found the key!
Why did it take so long to learn?
I've found how to get you back
The key for all concerned!

There are actually two methods
Who would have thought?
One I prefer to the other
But both work, so to either I'll resort!

One - open arms out wide
Call out with merry glee
Bop down rather low
Whilst calling out for thee!

The sillier I sound
The more amused you seem
The faster you return to me
And we're both relieved!

Treats also seem to work
That's option number two
The rustle of a packet
Seems to break your deafness through!

The moral of my story?
Leave all pride and dignity at the gate
When you take out your terrier
It'll solve any issues you can rate!

The Importance of a Sense of Humour

Well you've gone and done it
I didn't think you could
You have quite surpassed yourself
To be fair, you said you would!
I didn't think it possible
Such mess could be made
But as it turns out
That mess is easily laid
The bin can be overturned
And spread about the room
Your bed does indeed explode
With an apparent boom!
Toys can be shredded
With untold delight
And all within
One short and lonely night!
You'd think I would have heard it?
Been disturbed by such distress?
But like a silent thief
You destroy with such finesse!
Of course, I am angry
But there's no point, you see
Because you are adorable
And I forgive you easily!
It is not done with malice
I'm sure you were trying to help
Maybe there was some danger there
And I didn't hear your yelp?
Well, it is done now
And I still love your company
Which is a jolly good job
As you smell like a piggery!
You really are a funny one
Your smile will conquer all
Never a wrong move
Just a misguided call!
Let's go get breakfast
And start our day
I heard there are lots of adventures
Waiting for you, what do you say?

Last Laugh

On the odd occasion
I manage to win
To get in a little joke
That you didn't see comin'

I have to make mental note
And smile to myself
As I know you won't leave
My victory long on the shelf!

Retribution will be had
The last word, will be yours
The joke, will soon be on me
And you'll be laughing, of course!

But I'll take my victory
For the moment while I can!
And revel in the idea
That in charge, I *actually* am!

Together

You wag your tail
With a beaming smile aside
A silent communication
Of mutual love and pride
No words are necessary
For we both know
All is well together
Our love together grows

Companion

I have no idea which way I am going
What life holds for me today
Where I'll be tomorrow
Or what I want to say
But you walk beside me
Through adventure thick and thin
So everything will be alright
Regardless of the mischief we get in

4. THE INDIVIDUAL

The Individual

Don't expect us to act the same
For each to be as the next
As I can guarantee
There is a surprise waiting for you yet!

You can describe as a collective
But remember we're unique
And all my friends have
Their own particular mystique

Some like to play together
Some like to be alone
Mostly a mixture of both
But we'll soon let you know!

Why not consider
A few characteristics today
Just remember
You can't order us to be your way!

The Independent

Affection is well and all
But everything has its time
I enjoy it as much as anyone
But my independence is sublime!
My presence, itself is affection
The occasional, gentle nod
Or a good chin scratch
That'll do the job!
I don't want to sit on you
As you watch TV
But I'll always be *beside* you
Watching out, you'll see!

The Cuddler

My day is not complete
Unless it ends with a hug
I may require more
Even if you're holding a mug!
Everything comes second
Second, to the likes of me
As our enjoyment *is*
Completed by cuddling, you'll see!

The Comedian

Life is but a joke
And I must have my fun
I will not be serious
Not for anyone!
There are games to be invented
Amusement is not a fad
Join in my adventure
If not, you'll wish you had!

The Dedicated

I hide my head
In the sand
Or in a hedgerow
I don't give a damn!

Even if I get pricked
I must stop and stare
There may be critters
Lurking in there!

None shall get past me!
No, not today!
Not while *I'm* on guard!
Not while I play!

The Lazy

I have little intention
Of completing extra steps
Why? that is unnecessary!
I just, cannot accept!
There cannot be any need
In running so today?!
A gentle potter, then lunch
Is quite enough, I'd say!

The Gamer

My day is not complete
Unless I have my ball
None other will do
I don't want one for all!

Games must be plentiful
For happiness to reign
And so, I can dream happily!
For the rest of the day

The Bull

I have no patience
I have no time for that
Too many joys are waiting
And birds ready to be made flap

I will risk all
To achieve a thrill
Ever ready for adventure
Why on earth, should I sit still?!

The Observer

I stop and listen
I do not run in headfirst
There are many things around me
Some I love, some I dread, some worse

There is no need to charge in
To begin, I must observe all
Not ruin the surprise
On those I wish to call!

Patience is my virtue
Observation is key
Consider all around
And strike just when I please!

The Day Dreamer

I'll be there in a minute
But I'll think a while today
And consider all that may be
And what I want to say
Or what are *you* thinking?
I'll meditate on that
Before any action
I'll dream about a nap!

The Defender

I am on guard always
No one will get past me
Don't even try it
You'll not pass for free

My home is my castle
My people are my pride
No one will disrespect me
Or take me for a ride!

The Hunter

I am a hunter
Look out if you're my prey
I give fair warning
So, run away!

Run for me please
Yes, if you will
I don't mind
It's such a thrill

I love to chase
You all around
Or to stalk
And take you down

That's not nice
I hear you say?
But I was bred to hunt
That *is* my way!

Water Baby

I love to swim in water
Wherever it may be
Whether a stream, lake or river
Or even by the sea

I love to swim and splash
I love how it feels
I like to retrieve a ball
I will do this with great zeal

But I'm not always fussy
If none of the above are about
I'll gladly jump in a puddle
If its muddy, you do shout!

But I just love water
A paddling pool is nice
But if none of these are available
A water bowl will suffice!

The Thief

If you leave it unattended
Then that makes it mine
If you just dropped it
I will save the need to whine

If you look away
Or even leave the room
No longer pay attention
Then... BOOM!!

Yes, I claim it!
It is now all mine
Possession *is* the key
And I got there, just in time!

The Good, The Bad and The Ugly

Well, you can stop waiting for the ugly
I'll tell you that for free!
There's no such thing as an ugly terrier
No, ma'am, not me!

There may be things, you don't like
We'll call them 'the bad'
But really, I am true to myself
And that doesn't make me a cad!

A dog is no human
Our right and wrong ain't the same
So maybe don't condemn us
And try to pass the blame?

Our world is different
Our language, instinct and ways
We take *you* on as you are
How about *you* do the same?

We may hunt things you don't like
We may revel in the kill
But this is our nature
Not an expression of evil

We squabble and bicker
But you lot do the same
We're just more open
And don't secretly call out names

Our loyalty is unquestioning
Our love forever pure
Our cheek undeniable
But *that* you do adore!

Take us, as we are!
That's what we do to you!
So, how about we go for a walk
And find something new?

5. EXPLAINING LIFE TO YOUR HUMAN

You Say

You say 'enough'
I say 'that can't be'
My work is *never* done
Oh, when will you see?!

I do my best to protect you
To alert to what might befall
If you do not look out
And heed my warning call!

I'd say you are ungrateful
But an artist's work is rarely known
Or truly appreciated
Until many seeds are sown!

So, I will continue
To warn you everyday
Of the many perils
That surround us, in every way!

Contemplation

I lay here
And contemplate
And digest
What I just ate

All round
Are having fun
But I don't feel
The need to run

Here I lay
And contemplate
Happy to digest
All I ate

When everyone around me
Is as busy as a bee
I can't be bothered
Don't try to wind up me

I'm just contemplating
Life as it goes by
Others can run about
But why should I?

But while I'm here
For you I have a task
It's not difficult
Not a big ask!

Just bend down
And rub my tum
That is
My kind of fun!

Newborn

I lay around
On my back
Cute and chubby
Growing fat
Nothing around
Bothers me
For I am but
A newborn puppy

Others may
Run around
But I'll just sleep
And not make a sound
All is well
While I sleep
And dream of milk
And don't make a peep

I have no woes
To bother me
I am warm
And loved you see
Milk is here
Whenever I need
So really nothing
Worries me

In good time
I will run
And make more
Active fun
But for now
I'm in no rush
There's plenty of time
So please just hush

Foot Warmer

Occasionally I like to sit
And watch the world go by
Observing all around me
A peaceful use of time

But whilst doing so
To make my task complete
I ensure you are there
By sitting on your feet

Then you can't go anywhere
I know exactly where you are
Together we observe the world
Whether near or far

When we have both finished
We can continue on our way
Always together
That is a perfect day!

Impressive

You can try and catch me
But I hate to disappoint
I am the fastest terrier
You'll see about this joint!

Others try to catch me
Ha, if only they can!
But I am the fastest terrier
You'll see in this land!

I am quite impressive
None can stride like me
I am quick and nimble
Impressed? You should be!

The Dare

I bop and weave
It's such fun!
Try to catch me
Watch me run!

Join me, won't you?
There's room for two
Try to catch me!
I dare you!

A Simple Request

Ah, if I may
Quickly address?
The problem that
Is causing me stress!

You have the solution
In your grasp
It is but
A simple task

The smell that
Is bothering me
Needs a conclusion
Yes, indeed!

It's coming from your
Coat pocket
Such a whiff
I can't block it!

It's driving me
To distraction
And causing a
Surprising reaction

For you seem
To not understand
The solution is
But in *your* hand!

Will you please!
Reach into
Your coat pocket –
Happiness, will ensue!

For I know
What lies within
Don't pretend
It's in the tin

Hurry up!
I'm doing good
And performing
As I should

I've asked you nicely
More than once
So it's time
I came up trumps!

The Crumb

When scent of a crumb reaches me
It fills me with delight
As soon as I sniff it out
I know it will be alright

Crumbs come in various sizes
But I will find them all
Obviously the larger the better
But I'm not too proud for the small

I'm not fussy as to taste or texture
Prelicked or quite fresh
As long as it smells good to me
I'll absolutely do my best

I'll tidy up behind you
Be as messy as you like!
I am your mobile cleaner
Ever ready when crumbs do strike!

Resistance Is Futile

You can try
To resist
And not feed me
But I'll persist!

You can try
To pretend
Not to give in
But in the end

You can try
To insist
That your will
Will resist

You know
You can't resist!
And you'll feed me!
Yes, I *do* insist!

But we know
In the end
You *will* feed me
Yes, my friend!

I see you eating
It's not fair
My food is boring
You should really share

Resistance is futile
Haven't you heard?
What's mine is yours
To hoard, is absurd

I will gladly
Share mine with you
I suggest
You do the same too

Comfy

I thank you for my new bed
It is rather sweet
But do not be offended
If I prefer to sit at your feet

Or next to my bed
Or on the bare floor
Or indeed the concrete
That one I adore!

Don't feel bad
If you do not understand
The choice of my position
All *is* at hand!

Don't be confused
When I'm up against the wall
Or half in, half out of bed
That's the best position of all!

It may look uncomfortable
But it's all the same to me
I find it blissful
I'm as comfy as can be!

Sunshine

I sit and soak
Up the rays
As they beam down
I feel ok

As the sun shines
I feel well
Look at me glow
Can't you tell?

I love the sun
The sun loves me
Together the day
Brings harmony

Red Faced

I cannot tell how mad you are
But your face has gone quite red
And you're starting to spout the words
Most canines come to dread

So, I'll just go to my bed
With my tail between my legs
I do not think you meant to say
Half the mean words you said!

How was I supposed to know
Those were in fact new shoes?
That the tv remote was not a toy
And that dinner wasn't mine to choose?

If you leave things in my reach
Then that is my 'OK'
To help myself to whatever
Happens to come my way

My breeder told you how we are
But did you heed her call?
No, you smiled and said
"She's too cute to be naughty at all!"

Well, you had fair warning!
So, I have nothing else to say
It is all your fault
So just accept, it is how I play!

Maybe I have one last thing
On which I'd like to sing
Terriers rule, we do no wrong!
Ha! And we'll always win!

Mud

I just want
To give you a kiss
A chance for this
Should not be missed

I don't care
If I'm covered in mud
I just want
To show some love

I think we
Both agree?
A little mud
Won't hurt thee

So, come on Mum
Show me some love!
Afterall
It is *just* mud!

Shake It Down

I shake it down
To take it down
That is my way
I do not take prisoners
That ain't the terrier way!

Everything needs shaking
Anything that moves
Or if it didn't on its own
I've still got something to prove!

Shake it
Awake it
Throw it all around
I am a terrier!
I know not any bounds!

Helper

I bring you toys in the morning.
I'll even bring your shoe
So there can be no doubt
What you're supposed to do

See, I am just helping
You to start your day
See, the day has started!
It's time you're on your way

You need to get up
It's time to let me out
I need my breakfast
It's time you were about!

Frisbee

What is this thing called frisbee?
This little rubbery disc?
Oh, how I love to chase it
And give it a terrier kiss!

It glides through the air with style
I watch it fly with pride
I follow it with speed and precision
And trace it eagle-eyed

I'll catch it in mid air
Just before it falls
The wind may try to steal it
But I'll claim it after all

I will return it to you
With speed and delight
Ready for my frisbee
To again take its flight

No To Toads

I love to chase all creatures
No matter if great or small
Birds, cats or beetles
I will go after them all

But I have learnt my lesson
When it comes to toad and frog
For they taste rather foul
And make me froth from my gob

That really is unpleasant
It makes me feel quite sick
Apparently, it can be poisonous
So I won't touch 'em with a stick

Indeed, I've learnt a lesson
Not all creatures are for fun
Some I will let walk on by
But I'll make the next one run!

The Branch Manager

I trot along so happily
With my new found branch
I upgraded from a twig
It was too small to make a lance

It could not impress anyone
Or reach anything at all
So searched for another
And hoped a big one did fall

I was pleased when I found this
For now, I can trot along
And see how many friends
With it I can swiftly prong

I don't aim to damage
Just maybe give a bruise
Let everyone be impressed
As from behind I do cruise!

Yes, that's right, my intentions
Are a little bad
But I can't say I'm sorry
Or that I feel sad

For I just got a big crowd
As I trotted by
And now feel rather proud
You might ask me *why!?!*

I started with a low estimate
But now I want more from my stick
I'm glad I upgraded to a branch
A little heavier, a little thick

It's good fun to trot on by
And have all revel at me
A cheeky, feisty terrier
You best watch out for me!

The More The Merrier

How many terriers
Should be in your pack
Really depends
On if you lack
Time and space
Money too
Is your sense of humour
Large enough for two?

If you answer
'Yes' to all
Then by all means
Add more to your hall!
But remember
Twice the fun
Is not always right
For everyone!

Sometimes one
Is quite enough
Though stopping there
Can be tough!
As addictive
We can be
And a merry group
Is more fun, you see?!

And who is to say?
Two, three or four
Is more difficult
If you truly adore
All about us
And can say
'Life is better
With more today!'

Angelic

We walk this earth
With twice the heart
We live so true
From the very start

We live for less time
Because we get it right from the start
We need less than humans
So knowledge to you, we'll impart!

Though no one said
Angels could not walk with cheek
In equal measure
To also, being meek!

Where on earth
Would be the fun in that?
If we didn't also
Teach value in being a brat!?

We teach you humour
We show you love
We walk beside you
Our family is like a glove

Together we fit
Come what may
No matter what
Others may say

So, though I leave you
Before your time
Know that I'll always be there
With you, by your side

Terrier Spirit
Knows no bounds
In life and love
None better can be found!

So listen to me
As I pray
Know life is better
For knowing me today

Mon Amour

My legs may be creaking
My ears are nearly deaf
But there's value in this old man
I've wisdom for you yet

Our days together
Have been filled with love and fun
A partnership together
A race that's worth the run

I know one day I'll leave you
My time is coming near
But I'll always be with you
In our hearts we're always dear

I'll leave a gaping hole in the home
Of that there is no doubt
But you must have another terrier
Please, hear my reason out

For you must have another
Someone else to walk beside
Otherwise who will guard you
Or save your sorry hide?

You need someone to listen
To your tales of woe
To share in your joys
Exercise and keep you on your toes!

Continue on our journey
I'll walk with you evermore
In spirit and in purpose
Our love will last, Mon Amour!

6. CONCLUSIONS

The Question

Just when I think
Things can't get worse
You like to remind me
There are new things in the universe

Things can come in threes
Or multiples of them with you
You take great pride
In knocking me down a peg or two

No one will call me arrogant
While you are around
I'm sure you were sent to keep me humble
And my feet firmly on the ground

To educate me in patience
To leave all pride at your feet
And somehow, I still glow with joy
When people love you, when we meet?!

How on earth do you do it?
I'd *really* love to know!
How can you be so annoying?
But the most loveable creature I know?!

The Answer

Ah, my dear, I'm glad you asked
But secrets I can't tell!
You will just have to assume
That I do all things well!

Mostly I'm just misunderstood
My motives should be clear
But not everybody it would seem
Shares what I hold dear!

I've said it oh, so many times
By now you should really know
I live my life with cheek and charm
And through the laughter, my love shows

What you call 'annoying'
I call that quite 'quaint'
A little bit of feisty joy
Served up on your plate

Take a serving, won't you?
I'll wash away anything on which we disagree
Remember life would be so boring
If it wasn't shared with me!

Empathy

Do not just try to teach your dog
To understand what you want to say
How about you stop and think
What they might want today?

Try to have some empathy
Consider what they want
Stop and listen for a moment
Their voice might just haunt

Look a little closer
Behind those soulful eyes
There, waiting for you
Is a big surprise

They understand our meaning
Long before we say
Our mood forever reading
On the best and worst of day

They learn our language
Comprehending more than you know
Translating so many gestures
That you don't know you show

They understand time
And don't need a clock
They know what makes us tick
Can you say the same or do you just mock?

Do you understand them?
Appreciate for who they are?
Or try to repress
Like a Victorian bra?

Let your dog flourish
Do not repress
Their ability and understanding
It's amazing and should only impress

They know what is passing
Even if they do not speak
How about you stop and listen
Empathy doesn't make you weak

Their ways are different
Human is not the same as hound
But it doesn't have to follow
That there is no common ground

And that which is different
Doesn't make them bad
Or in need of changing
That would only make them sad

We are not so superior
Our intellect is not supreme
There is much understanding
If only you would gleam

So look a little harder
Stop and consider today
How your dog is feeling
And what they're trying to say

Reflections

Sometimes I see you
Scrutinising me
No one should ever doubt
You understand what you see

They should observe that look
The look that you give
When clearly examining me
And thoughts do outlive

You are trying to convey
Hoping that I see
That the message, is not lost
Lost on the likes of me!

Am I paying attention?
Do I understand?
If only I'd get with it
And understand your plan!

For you have a message
It is coming clear
For anyone who cares
To watch, listen or adhere

Canine communication
Silent, some may be
But there are words nonetheless
If only you would see!

See the body language
The direction of the stare
What they are pointing at
Who, what or where!

So, pay attention!
To what they are trying to say
Chances are, there is some wisdom
In your canine today!

Of course, they might just want a ball
Or to have some fun
To receive attention
Or to show what they've just won

But actually, there is wisdom
In sharing all their joys
In giving them a cuddle
Or sharing with their toys

Open up your heart
Let your spirit be
And you might just find
The wisdom in front of thee!

Blessing

If anyone uses the word 'just'
Before they say 'a dog'
Then *just* walk away
And leave them agog
There is nothing you can do for them
Their heart is made of stone
They do not understand or deserve the love
That knowing a dog shows
The loyalty and affection
The friendship ever true
The comedy and amusement
The companion when you're blue
The never failing presence
Through every step in life
The family member that stands beside
Any man or wife
They'll see you through thick and thin
Through every laugh or sigh
A shadow never changing
Throughout all their lives
An enrichment that cannot be
Truly reasoned or explained
Why life with a canine is
A blessing beyond any name

I do

When you take on a terrier
Or any animal at all
It is similar to marriage vows
So be prepared for all that calls
For there will be days of trial
For sadness but also joy
For tests of patience
And demand for new toys!

New ones will get eaten
Or ripped and left about the room
Destruction left for all to see
As toys meet their doom
So I wouldn't count on riches
They're happy if you're poor
As long as you're with them
And your love, you do outpour

I'd get vet insurance
As that's another test
On your finances
I said they'd do their best
To spend all your money
On things that they need
But they will repay you
With more than you can conceive

They will share you
With other members of family
They can have two legs or four
This is their decree
To love and cherish
All the days on God's earth
In sickness and health
For better and worse

They will see you
Through every single day
And teach you your value
And the value of a time of play
Cherish them forever
Laugh, love and care
Till that dark day
When heaven no longer shares

That day will tear you
I can't say otherwise
But take comfort in knowing
An angel walked beside
Your heart has a shadow
That can't be replaced
But a void can be filled
With a new angel face

Blessings continue
Canine love all divine
Heartache worth knowing
As it opens love beyond this time

The Honour

The privilege that comes
At witnessing a birth
Is something quite remarkable
Like nothing else on Earth

The miracle that happens
Each and every time
As a newborn arrives into this world
Really is sublime

I experience an extra honour
Of the like, there is none else
For when it's my girls time
They don't leave me on the shelf

They actively ask for me
Their experience to share
To help and hold their paw
And lend a hand with care

The honour in that moment
Of realisation of our bond
Is something quite remarkable
A knowing we belong

I'd never miss those moments
The honour, it is all mine
But so is the responsibility
In insuring that honour does shine

For I must do my upmost
To insure that all life
Is honoured and respected
And birth is without strife

That isn't always easy
For not everything goes to plan
But my pledge is to always be there
And do everything I can

And not just in that moment
But every one that succeeds
Both whilst under my direct care
And as new families supersede

For that is the honour and the privilege
Any breeder worth a damn
Takes upon their shoulders
Before any breeding plan

For it is planned, not luck
Not that dog A and dog B
Happened to have cute pups
And all ended happily

But by time, care and love
Each pairing is designed
Health and character are matched
And passed down the lines

So, the honour and privilege
Is all absolutely mine
To live and breathe a terrier partnership
Is wholly divine

Crazy Dog Lady

Some call me crazy
They're probably quite right
I really don't mind it
I'll own the title, that's alright!

I think I am quite crazy
In fact, I must be
To live with a pack of terriers
Says a lot about me!

Though I prefer 'unique' or 'eccentric'
It doesn't matter much
A 'crazy dog lady'
Just means I have been touched

By the charm that is terrier
And that is fine by me
If others don't appreciate?
Well, that doesn't worry me!

But I will own it!
And crazy be
For life with a pack of terriers
Is certainly the life for me!

Photo credit: Sergio Muelle